Formula One Trivia Quiz Book

500 Questions on Grand Prix Greats

Chris Bradshaw

Front cover image created by headfuzz by grimboid. Check out his great collection of TV, movie and sport-themed posters online at:

https://www.etsy.com/shop/headfuzzbygrimboid

Introduction

Think you know about the Formula 1? Put your knowledge to the test with this collection of quizzes on Grand Prix greats.

The book covers the whole history of Formula 1, from the earliest races on to the wild 1970s and 80s through to the present day.

The biggest names in motor racing history are present and correct so look out for questions on Lewis Hamilton, Max Verstappen, Nigel Mansell, Ayrton Senna, Michael Schumacher and many, many more.

There are 500 questions in all covering teams and drivers, circuits and strategy and much else besides.

Each quiz contains a selection of 20 questions and is either a mixed bag of pot luck testers or is centred on a specific category such as the British Grand Prix or the 1990s.

There are easy, medium and hard questions offering something for F1 novices as well as professors of Grand Prix history.

You'll find the answers to each quiz below the bottom of the following quiz. For example, the answers to Quiz 1: Pot Luck, are underneath Quiz 2: Lewis Hamilton. The only exception is Quiz 25: Pot Luck. The answers to these can be found under the Quiz 1 questions.

We hope you enjoy the Formula One Trivia Quiz Book.

About the Author

Chris Bradshaw has written more than 30 quiz books including titles for Britain's biggest selling daily newspaper, The Sun, and The Times (of London). In addition to the NFL, he has written extensively on soccer, cricket, darts and poker.

He lives in Birmingham, England and has been following motor racing for over 30 years.

Acknowledgements

Many thanks to Ken and Veronica Bradshaw, Heidi Grant, Steph, James, Ben and Will Roe and Graham Nash.

CONTENTS

Quiz 1: Pot Luck

1. Which two drivers are the co-holders of the record for the most World Drivers' Championship wins?

2. What flag is waved to signify the end of a Grand Prix race?

3. Who won his first Drivers' Championship in 2021?

4. Who is the youngest winner of the World Drivers' Championship?

5. Since 2011 Formula One has exclusively used tyres made by which manufacturer?

6. In what decade was the Williams team founded?

7. Michael Schumacher won his first two World Drivers' Championships with which team?

8. Who won the South African Grand Prix in 1983 then had to wait a record six years and 211 days to win his second race in San Marino in 1990?

9. Who drives in Formula One in the #5 car?

10. What Grand Prix is staged at the Yas Marina circuit?

11. Which Grand Prix makes up part of motor sport's 'Triple Crown' alongside the Indy 500 and 24 Hours of Le Mans?

12. Who is the only driver to have won all three legs of the 'Triple Crown'?

13. Who was the oldest driver in the 2022 Formula One season?

14. What was the opening Grand Prix of the 2022 season?

15. What are the four circuits that hosted races in the first ever Formula One World Championship season that are still on the calendar today?

16. Which Formula One driver went on to win three gold medals at the 2012 and 2016 Paralympics in handcycling?

17. Who was the last Williams driver to win a Grand Prix?

18. Which constructor has had two of its cars on the front row of the grid the most times?

19. Due to terrible weather conditions, the shortest ever Grand Prix race took place in 2021 at which circuit? a) Monza b) Silverstone c) Spa

20. What distance was covered in that historic short race? a) 6.88km 16.88km c) 26.88km

Quiz 25: Answers

1. Sir Jackie Stewart 2. Max Verstappen 3. The Red Sea 4. Northamptonshire 5. Mario Andretti 6. Alpine 7. Thursday 8. Alain Prost 9. Nürburgring 10. Texas 11. New Zealand 12. Frank Williams 13. True 14. Jerez 15. Sergio Perez 16. 5ft 1in 17. Lewis Hamilton 18. Sir Jackie Stewart 19. c) 18in 20. a) Black and white diagonals

Quiz 2: Lewis Hamilton

1. Hamilton started his Formula One career driving for which team?

2. Who pipped Hamilton to the Drivers' Championship by one point in his debut season?

3. Hamilton secured his first Grand Prix win in 2007 in which race?

4. How old was Hamilton when he won his first Grand Prix?

5. Which driver did Hamilton overtake on the last lap of the last race of the 2008 season to secure his first Drivers' Championship?

6. Hamilton secured that maiden title at which race?

7. True or false – Hamilton was the first driver to win 100 Grands Prix?

8. What colour helmet did Hamilton wear for the 2022 season?

9. Who controversially threw his cap at Hamilton after the Englishman claimed the 2016 US Grand Prix?

10. Hamilton won his first World Championship in just his second season in Formula One. Who is the only other driver to manage that feat?

11. Hamilton holds the record for the most career pole positions. Whose record did he break?

12. Hamilton has won the British Grand Prix and what other race a record eight times?

13. In 2018, Hamilton won which Grand Prix despite starting in 14th place on the grid?

14. Hamilton won the World Drivers' Championship every year between 2014 and 2020 bar one. Who won the title in 2016?

15. Who was the last Briton before Hamilton to win the World Drivers' Championship?

16. True or false – Hamilton is an investor in a vegan restaurant chain called Neat Burger?

17. Hamilton won which race every year between 2017 and 2021?

18. Hamilton was born and raised in which Hertfordshire town?

19. In 2014, Hamilton set a record after recording pole position, winning the race and leading on every lap of the race in which Grand Prix? a) Belgian b) Hungarian c) Malaysian

20. Hamilton holds the record for the most consecutive Formula One starts with how many? a) 245 b) 255 c) 265

Quiz 1: Answers

1. Lewis Hamilton and Michael Schumacher 2. Chequered flag 3. Max Verstappen 4. Sebastian Vettel 5. Pirelli 6. 1970s 7. Benetton 8. Riccardo Patrese 9. Sebastian Vettel 10. Abu Dhabi 11. Monaco 12. Graham Hill 13. Fernando Alonso 14. Bahrain 15. Silverstone, Monaco, Spa and Monza 16. Alex Zanardi 17. Pastor Maldonado 18. Mercedes 19. c) Spa 20. a) 6.88km

Quiz 3: Pot Luck

1. Who made his F1 debut in 1980 but didn't win his first World Drivers' Championship until 1992?

2. What was the first constructor to start over 1,000 races?

3. Alpine is the motorsport arm of which giant auto manufacturer?

4. Which Spanish city hosted the European Grand Prix from 2008 through to 2012?

5. In relation to motorsport, what do the initials BRDC stand for?

6. What colour flag is flown to warn drivers of a hazard on or close to the track?

7. 'To Hell and Back' was the title of which World Champion's autobiography?

8. Which driver finally reached the podium at the 2019 Brazilian Grand Prix after a record 101 starts out of the top three?

9. Michael Schumacher got his big break in Formula One after which French driver was jailed following an altercation with a London taxi driver?

10. Who are the two father/son tandems to have won the World Drivers' Championship?

11. How many points are awarded to the driver who achieves the fastest lap in a Grand Prix?

12. Which British F1 driver co-created a brand of aftershave called 'Pole Position'?

13. True or false – Lewis Hamilton appeared on children's TV show 'Blue Peter' at the age of seven, racing radio-controlled cars?

14. Which driver chose to drive in the #10 car as a tribute to French footballer Zinedine Zidane?

15. True or false – Kevin Magnussen worked as a welder in a factory before becoming a racing driver?

16. Who holds the record for the most Grand Prix starts by a British driver without a win?

17. In 1979, which driver gave Williams their first Grand Prix win?

18. Who was the last driver before Max Verstappen to win the World Drivers' Championship in a car with a Honda engine?

19. The shortest Formula One race to go its full distance lasted how long? a) 64 minutes b) 74 minutes c) 84 minutes

20. That record race was the 2003 edition of which Grand Prix? a) British Grand Prix b) Italian Grand Prix c) Monaco Grand Prix

Quiz 2: Answers

1. McLaren 2. Kimi Räikkönen 3. Canadian Grand Prix 4. 22 years old 5. Timo Glock 6. Brazilian Grand Prix 7. True 8. Yellow 9. Nico Rosberg 10. Jacques Villeneuve 11. Ayrton Senna's 12. Hungarian 13. German Grand Prix 14. Nico Rosberg 15. Damon Hill 16. True 17. Spanish Grand Prix 18. Stevenage 19. c) Malaysian 20. c) 265

Quiz 4: F1 Legends

1. Who was the first winner of the World Drivers' Championship?

2. Who was the first man to win the World Championship in three consecutive years?

3. Who was Britain's first World Drivers' Champion?

4. Who is the only man to have won World Championships in both Formula One and on motorcycles?

5. Who was the first driver to reach the milestone of 50 Grand Prix wins?

6. Excluding Michael Schumacher, who was the last Ferrari driver to win the World Drivers' Championship more than once?

7. Who are the two drivers to have won 13 races in a single season?

8. Which legend gained pole position in almost 56% of the races he competed in?

9. Who is the only driver to make the podium in every race he appeared in in a single season?

10. Ayrton Senna won all three of his World Championships at which circuit?

11. Which World Champion was an aerospace engineer before concentrating on his driving career?

12. Who was the first Briton to win the World Drivers' Championship more than once?

13. Who was the first Brazilian to win a hat-trick of World Drivers' Championship titles?

14. Who is the only Finn to have won the World Drivers' Championship more than once?

15. Who is the oldest man to win the World Drivers' Championship?

16. Which multiple World Champion said, "You cannot always be the best. But you can do your best."?

17. Michael Schumacher won which race a record eight times between 1994 and 2006?

18. Who was the last British driver to win the World Championship while driving a Ferrari?

19. Who had to wait a record seven seasons between winning his second and third World Drivers' Championships? a) Graham Hill b) Niki Lauda c) Nelson Piquet

20. Who holds the record for setting the fastest lap the most times in the history of Formula One? a) Lewis Hamilton b) Michael Schumacher c) Sebastian Vettel

Quiz 3: Answers

1. Nigel Mansell 2. Ferrari 3. Renault 4. Valencia 5. British Racing Drivers' Club 6. Yellow 7. Niki Lauda 8. Carlos Sainz 9. Bertrand Gachot 10. Graham and Damon Hill and Keke and Nico Rosberg 11. One 12. David Coulthard 13. True 14. Pierre Gasly 15. True 16. Martin Brundle 17. Clay Regazonni 18. Ayrton Senna 19. b) 74 minutes 20. b) Italian Grand Prix

Quiz 5: Pot Luck

1. Who holds the record for the most starts in the history of Formula One?

2. Which British driver was the owner of the Team UK Youth cycling team?

3. In 2021, who became just the third driver to qualify in the top 10 in 100 consecutive races?

4. Who are the other two drivers to manage that century of successive top 10 qualifications?

5. Which constructor has the most race wins in the history of the Formula One Championship?

6. What colour flag is waved to indicate a session has been suspended and that drivers should reduce speed and return to the pit lane?

7. Which Grand Prix takes place at the Albert Park Circuit?

8. In 1975, who became the first woman to score a World Championship point?

9. Which Ferrari driver finished in 7th, 7th, 6th, 5th and 5th in the World Drivers' Championship in the early 1990s?

10. True or false – The 1991 Australian Grand Prix lasted just 24 minutes?

11. Which British driver's autobiography was called 'What Doesn't Kill You...'?

12. Which Italian failed to reach the finish line on 18 straight occasions not once but twice in his F1 career?

13. Which French former F1 driver is a budding chef who penned a cook book called 'Cuisine and Confidences'?

14. During the 2022 season, the top how many finishers in each race were awarded points?

15. Fernando Alonso drives in what number car?

16. Who was the first British driver to win the BBC Sports Personality of the Year Award more than once?

17. True or false – Romain Grosjean is the brother of former world #4 tennis star Sebastian Grosjean?

18. Who was the last man to win the World Drivers' Championship whose full name starts and ends with the same letter?

19. What is the longest circuit on the 2022 F1 calendar? a) Baku b) Silverstone c) Spa

20. How long is a lap on that circuit? a) 5.004km b) 6.004km c) 7.004km

Quiz 4: Answers

1. Giuseppe Farina 2. Juan Manuel Fangio 3. Mike Hawthorn 4. John Surtees 5. Alain Prost 6. Niki Lauda 7. Michael Schumacher and Sebastian Vettel 8. Juan Manuel Fangio 9. Michael Schumacher 10. Suzuka 11. Nigel Mansell 12. Jim Clark 13. Nelson Piquet 14. Mika Häkkinen 15. Juan Manuel Fangio 16. Sebastian Vettel 17. French Grand Prix 18. John Surtees 19. b) Niki Lauda 20. b) Michael Schumacher

Quiz 6: Nicknames

1. The Professor
2. The Iceman
3. Il Leone
4. The Rat
5. The Honey Badger
6. Britney
7. The Monza Gorilla
8. The Bear
9. The Shunt
10. Maestro
11. Crashtor
12. Johnny Carwash
13. The Red Baron
14. Billion Dollar Man
15. Mad Max
16. The Finger
17. Mr. Monaco

A. Nigel Mansell
B. Vittorio Brambilla
C. Pastor Maldonado
D. James Hunt
E. Michael Schumacher
F. Graham Hill
G. Alain Prost
H. Sebastian Vettel
I. Max Verstappen
J. Daniel Ricciardo
K. Lewis Hamilton
L. Sergio Perez
M. Niki Lauda
N. Juan Manuel Fangio
O. Gilles Villeneuve
P. Nico Rosberg
Q. Giovanni Lavaggi

18. The Aviator   R. Carlos Sainz

19. Checo   S. Kimi Räikkönen

20. Smooth Operator   T. Denny Hulme

Quiz 5: Answers

1. Kimi Räikkönen 2. Nigel Mansell 3. Valtteri Bottas 4. Alain Prost and Ayrton Senna 5. Ferrari 6. Red 7. Australian 8. Lella Lombardi 9. Jean Alesi 10. True 11. Johnny Herbert 12. Andrea De Cesaris 13. Romain Grosjean 14. Ten 15. #14 16. Nigel Mansell 17. False 18. Ayrton Senna 19. c) Spa 20. c) 7.004km

Quiz 7: Pot Luck

1. At the 2015 Australian Grand Prix, who became the youngest driver to start a race?

2. How old was that record-breaking driver?

3. Who is the only man to have won the World Drivers' Championship in five straight years?

4. Which Briton secured his first podium finish in his 91st race at the 1992 French Grand Prix?

5. What Grand Prix takes place at the Autódromo Hermanos Rodríguez?

6. What are the two countries to have hosted an F1 Grand Prix every year since 1950?

7. Which constructor won over 90% of races during the 2016 season?

8. Who is the only Formula One driver to win the BBC Sports Personality of the Year award who has never won the World Drivers' Championship?

9. Which World Champion's autobiography was called 'Life to the Limit'?

10. Which track is often shortened to COTA?

11. Who was the first British driver to start 300 Formula One races?

12. True or false – German F1 driver Timo Glock is a qualified scaffolding engineer?

13. Lewis Hamilton played schoolboy football alongside which England international (who was the first Englishman to have won Italy's Serie A and the Premier League)?

14. 'Unless I'm Very Much Mistaken' was the title of which Formula One figure's autobiography?

15. Who won the BBC Sports Personality of the Year Award in both 1994 and 1996?

16. Which driver's #77 car was the highest number on the 2022 Formula One grid?

17. Who was the last Brabham driver to win the World Championship?

18. True or false – The 1951 French Grand Prix was run over a distance of more than 600km?

19. What is the fastest pit stop in the history of Formula One? a) 1.82 seconds b) 1.92 seconds c) 2.02 seconds

20. Which team was responsible for that record-breaking pit stop? a) Ferrari b) McLaren c) Red Bull

Quiz 6: Answers

1. G) Alain Prost 2. S) Kimi Räikkönen 3. A) Nigel Mansell 4. M) Niki Lauda 5. J) Daniel Ricciardo 6. P) Nico Rosberg 7. B) Vittorio Brambilla 8. T) Denny Hulme 9. D) James Hunt 10. N) Juan Manuel Fangio 11. C) Pastor Maldonado 12. Q) Giovanni Lavaggi 13. E) Michael Schumacher 14. K) Lewis Hamilton 15. I) Max Verstappen 16. H) Sebastian Vettel 17. F) Graham Hill 18. O) Gilles Villeneuve 19. L) Sergio Perez 20. R) Carlos Sainz

Quiz 8: Best of British

1. Who was the first Briton to successfully defend the World Drivers' Championship?

2. Which Briton finished runner-up in the World Drivers' Championship for four straight seasons during the 1950s?

3. Lewis Hamilton holds the record for the most Grand Prix wins by a British driver. Who is second on that list?

4. Which Briton won the 1958 World Drivers' Championship despite winning just one race that season?

5. Which Briton won at least one race for seven straight seasons between 1997 and 2003?

6. Whose 70% race win rate in 1963 is the best in a single F1 season by a British driver?

7. Who is the oldest British driver to have won an F1 race?

8. Which British driver, who started more than 80 races during the 1980s, is a qualified medical doctor?

9. Who is the only driver to hold the F1 and CART championships at the same time?

10. Who are the two British drivers to have won a race in their first Formula One season?

11. Which Briton is the only driver to have raced in a car bearing the number 0?

12. Which British driver, who started 147 races between 1981 and 1993, enjoyed all four of his career podium finishes in 1984?

13. Which driver was fined $2,000 for punching a marshal at the 1977 Canadian Grand Prix?

14. Who is the youngest British driver to appear in a Formula One race?

15. Whose career included 13 race wins and 62 podium finishes but no World Championships?

16. Every race in Lewis Hamilton's F1 career has been in a car with an engine from which manufacturer?

17. Lewis Hamilton holds the record for the most consecutive races started by a British driver. Whose record did he break?

18. Which British great from the 1950s was known as 'The Racing Dentist'?

19. Lewis Hamilton is a part owner of which NFL team? a) Denver Broncos b) Kansas City Chiefs c) Las Vegas Raiders

20. Which British World Champion bred budgerigars after his retirement from F1? a) Damon Hill b) James Hunt c) Nigel Mansell

Quiz 7: Answers

1. Max Verstappen 2. 17 years old 3. Michael Schumacher 4. Martin Brundle 5. Mexico Grand Prix 6. Britain and Italy 7. Mercedes 8. Stirling Moss 9. Jenson Button 10. Circuit of the Americas 11. Jenson Button 12. True 13. Ashley Young 14. Murray Walker 15. Damon Hill 16. Valtteri Bottas 17. Nelson Piquet 18. True 19. a) 1.82 seconds 20. c) Red Bull

Quiz 9: Pot Luck

1. Which circuit was Nelson Piquet describing when he said, 'it's like riding a bicycle around your living room'?

2. The eGaming and apparel brand Quadrant was founded by which driver?

3. What colour flag is waved at a driver who is about to be lapped?

4. 15 of the 16 races during the 1988 season were won by drivers representing which team?

5. Which driver appeared on the 2018 Christina Aguilera song 'Pipe' using the pseudonym 'XNDA'?

6. From 1985 through to 1995 the Australian Grand Prix was hosted in which city?

7. True or false – The Silverstone circuit is located on a former Royal Air Force bomber base?

8. Who was the first man to win the World Drivers' Championship while driving for Williams?

9. The Autodromo Enzo e Dino Ferrari is the official name of which circuit?

10. Who holds the record for the most Formula One race starts before winning a first World Drivers' Championship?

11. Who became the first McLaren driver in nine years to win a Grand Prix after triumphing in Italy in 2021?

12. Who was the last McLaren driver before then to win a race?

13. Who was the only driver to win a race in 2021 who comes from a country that has a flag that includes a colour other than red, white or blue?

14. Which city in the American Midwest staged a Formula One Grand Prix every year from 1982 through to 1988?

15. Raced over 310km, the longest Grand Prix on the F1 calendar since 2000 has been which race?

16. At the 2012 Monaco Grand Prix, Kimi Raikkonen wore a specially designed helmet which honoured which former World Champion?

17. True or false – Sebastian Vettel is afraid of mice?

18. 'Watching the Wheels' was the title of which World Champion's autobiography?

19. Which country has produced the most Grand Prix race winners? a) Britain b) France c) Italy

20. What was the first Grand Prix to be hosted at night? a) Abu Dhabi b) Bahrain c) Singapore

Quiz 8: Answers

1. Lewis Hamilton 2. Stirling Moss 3. Nigel Mansell 4. Mike Hawthorn 5. David Coulthard 6. Jim Clark 7. Nigel Mansell 8. Jonathan Palmer 9. Nigel Mansell 10. Lewis Hamilton and Sir Jackie Stewart 11. Damon Hill 12. Derek Warwick 13. James Hunt 14. Lando Norris 15. David Coulthard 16. Mercedes 17. Jenson Button 18. Tony Brooks 19. a) Denver Broncos 20. b) James Hunt

Quiz 10: British Grand Prix

1. Which driver holds the record for the most British Grand Prix wins?

2. Which Spaniard won the 2022 British Grand Prix?

3. Who were the two Britons to win the race during the 1970s?

4. Who holds the record for the most wins in the British Grand Prix by a non-British driver?

5. Set in 2020, who holds the Silverstone British Grand Prix lap record?

6. Who was the first British winner of the British Grand Prix?

7. Excluding Silverstone, which circuit has hosted the British Grand Prix the most times?

8. Who holds the record for the most poles at the British Grand Prix?

9. What was the last circuit other than Silverstone to host the British Grand Prix?

10. Who overturned a 28-second deficit with just 29 laps left to win an amazing 1987 British Grand Prix?

11. Who was pipped at the post in that famous 1987 race?

12. Who ran out of fuel at the end of the 1991 British Grand Prix and was forced to grab a lift from Nigel Mansell?

13. The podiums at the British Grands Prix in 1963 and 1965 were all British affairs. Which three drivers filled the podium?

14. Who was the last non-European to win the race?

15. Which constructor has won the British Grand Prix the most times?

16. In 1951, who became the first South American to win the British Grand Prix?

17. Excluding Lewis Hamilton, who was the last driver to win the British Grand Prix in back-to-back seasons?

18. The 2022 British Grand Prix was run over how many laps?

19. Up to and including the 2022 race, how many British drivers have won their home Grand Prix? a) 10 b) 11 c) 12

20. How long is a lap of the Silverstone circuit? a) 4.891km b) 5.891km c) 6.891km

Quiz 9: Answers

1. Monaco 2. Lando Norris 3. Blue 4. McLaren 5. Lewis Hamilton 6. Adelaide 7. True 8. Alan Jones 9. Imola 10. Nico Rosberg 11. Daniel Ricciardo 12. Jenson Button 13. Sergio Perez 14. Detroit 15. Japanese Grand Prix 16. James Hunt 17. True 18. Damon Hill 19. a) Britain 20. c) Singapore

Quiz 11: Pot Luck

1. Whose 15 pole positions in 2011 are the most by a driver in a single season?

2. Who holds the record for the most wins at the Monaco Grand Prix?

3. Which Frenchman started his Formula One career in 2016 with a record 27 successive finishes?

4. What colour flag is held rather than waved and warns drivers about a change to the surface of the track like the addition of oil or water?

5. How many points are awarded to the winning driver in a Formula One race?

6. Which constructor won the Russian Grand Prix a record eight years in a row from 2014?

7. Which Australian was the first Formula One driver to be knighted?

8. What town in the Modena province of Italy is the home of Ferrari?

9. Lewis Hamilton secured his historic 100th Grand Prix win in 2021 at which race?

10. What number car does Daniel Ricciardo drive?

11. Which driver made a guest appearance as a guitarist on a song called 'Demolition Man' by Sheffield rockers Def Leppard?

12. At just 3.32km per lap, what is the shortest circuit on the Formula One calendar?

13. Which team won both the Drivers' Championship and the Constructors' Championship in both 2005 and 2006?

14. What is the only Scandinavian country to have hosted a Formula One Grand Prix?

15. The Brands Hatch circuit is in which English county?

16. Who is the only reigning British monarch to have watched the British Grand Prix in person?

17. 'Aussie Grit' was the title of which F1 driver's autobiography?

18. Who was the winner of the first Grand Prix hosted at night?

19. What is the fastest speed ever recorded during a Formula One race? a) 221.4 mph b) 231.4 mph c) 241.4 mph

20. Which driver set that record at the 2016 Mexico Grand Prix? a) Valtteri Bottas b) Nico Rosberg c) Sebastian Vettel

Quiz 10: Answers

1. Lewis Hamilton 2. Carlos Sainz 3. Jackie Stewart and James Hunt 4. Alain Prost 5. Max Verstappen 6. Stirling Moss 7. Brands Hatch 8. Lewis Hamilton 9. Brands Hatch 10. Nigel Mansell 11. Nelson Piquet 12. Ayrton Senna 13. Jim Clark, John Surtees and Graham Hill 14. Australia's Mark Webber 15. Ferrari 16. Jose Frolian Gonzalez 17. David Coulthard 18. 52 laps 19. c) 12 drivers 20. b) 5.891km

Quiz 12: Young Generation

1. During his debut Formula One season Max Verstappen drove for which team?

2. Verstappen made his debut for Red Bull as a replacement for which driver?

3. Who was the first driver to represent Thailand in Formula One?

4. Which driver secured his maiden Formula One victory at the 2021 Hungarian Grand Prix?

5. Which driver's car was flipped upside down and over the barriers following a massive crash at the 2022 British Grand Prix?

6. At the 2017 Azerbaijan Grand Prix, who became the youngest driver to achieve a podium finish in his rookie season?

7. True or false – Max Verstappen competed in Formula One before receiving his road driving licence?

8. Frenchman Pierre Gasly won his first Grand Prix driving for which team?

9. In 2021, who became the first Japanese driver in seven years to start a Formula One race?

10. Who is the youngest driver to start a Grand Prix from the front row of the grid?

11. Max Verstappen earned his first points in Formula One at which Asian Grand Prix?

12. True or false – Lando Norris was named after a character from the 'Star Wars' films?

13. Which Briton drives a car with the number 63?

14. Which young star recorded the fastest lap en route to a sixth-place finish at the 2022 Monaco Grand Prix despite suffering from tonsilitis?

15. Who are the two drivers to win points before their 19th birthday?

16. True or false – Mick Schumacher likes to prepare for a race by playing a game of chess?

17. Strulovitch is the real surname of which rising star?

18. Which young driver's seven pole positions in 2019 was the most that season?

19. Which of the following drivers wasn't a winner of the Formula 3 European Drivers' Championship before heading to Formula One? a) Lando Norris b) Lance Stroll c) Max Verstappen

20. In which English city was Lando Norris born and raised? a) Birmingham b) Bradford c) Bristol

Quiz 11: Answers

1. Sebastian Vettel 2. Ayrton Senna 3. Esteban Ocon 4. Red and yellow 5. 25 points 6. Mercedes 7. Sir Jack Brabham 8. Maranello 9. Russian Grand Prix 10. #3 11. Damon Hill 12. Monaco 13. Renault 14. Sweden 15. Kent 16. King George VI 17. Mark Webber 18. Fernando Alonso 19. b) 231.4 mph 20. a) Valtteri Bottas

Quiz 13: Pot Luck

1. How many points does the runner up receive in a Formula One race?

2. Who was the last driver to win back-to-back Monaco Grands Prix?

3. Which British constructor had 383 starts between 1978 and 2002 but never managed to win a race?

4. Which British circuit hosted the 1993 European Grand Prix?

5. Which former F1 driver won the Special Prize Entrepreneur of the Year at the 2018 GreenTec Awards?

6. Which Grand Prix is hosted at the Circuit Gilles Villeneuve?

7. A corner called 'Eau Rouge' is a famous feature of which circuit?

8. True or false – Seth Brundle, the main character in the cult movie 'The Fly' was named after F1 driver Martin Brundle?

9. Who was the first F1 driver to do a 'shoey' and celebrate a win by drinking champagne from his shoe?

10. True or false – No driver won back-to-back World Championships during the 1970s?

11. The Spa-Francorchamps circuit is situated within which famous forest?

12. Who drove the #1 car during the 2022 season?

13. Which driver reached the podium no fewer than 13 times between 2000 and 2011 but never won a Grand Prix?

14. The FIA is the governing body of motorsport. What do the initials FIA stand for?

15. Who is the main commentator on Sky Sports' Formula One coverage?

16. Who is the only Formula One driver to have been knighted who didn't win the World Drivers' Championship?

17. Which American city hosted its first Formula One Grand Prix in May 2022?

18. Who set the fastest lap for the first time in his 203rd race at the 2009 Bahrain Grand Prix?

19. Who holds the record for the most consecutive Grand Prix wins? a) Lewis Hamilton b) Ayrton Senna c) Sebastian Vettel

20. How many successive races did he win to set that record? a) seven b) eight c) nine

Quiz 12: Answers

1. Scuderia Toro Rosa 2. Daniil Kvyat 3. Alex Albon 4. Esteban Ocon 5. Zhou Guanyu 6. Lance Stroll 7. True 8. Alpha Tauri 9. Yuki Tsunoda 10. Lance Stroll 11. Malaysian 12. False 13. George Russell 14. Lando Norris 15. Max Verstappen and Lance Stroll 16. True 17. Lance Stroll 18. Charles Leclerc 19. c) Max Verstappen 20. c) Bristol

Quiz 14: 1970s

1. Which Briton won the World Drivers' Championship in 1971 and 1973?

2. Which Austrian became the sport's first posthumous World Champion in 1970?

3. Which constructor secured their first ever race win at the Spanish Grand Prix in 1971?

4. In 1972, who became the first Brazilian to win the World Drivers' Championship?

5. James Hunt made his Formula One debut in 1973 driving for which team?

6. Which two circuits hosted the British Grand Prix during the 1970s?

7. True or false – A record seven different drivers won the World Championship during the 1970s?

8. The 1979 song 'Faster' by George Harrison was recorded as a tribute to which driver who was tragically killed following a crash at the 1978 Italian Grand Prix?

9. The first Japanese Grand Prix was hosted in 1976 at a circuit overlooked by which mountain?

10. In 1979, who became the second Swiss driver to win the British Grand Prix?

11. Niki Lauda suffered a horrific crash in a 1976 race at which circuit?

12. In what year did James Hunt win his only World Drivers' Championship?

13. Hunt won that title while driving for which team?

14. Who were the three drivers to win multiple World Championships during the 1970s?

15. Which Canadian won the first of six Grands Prix at his home race in 1978?

16. In 1978, who became the second American to win the World Drivers' Championship?

17. In what year were slick tyres used in a Formula One race for the first time?

18. Which 38-year-old was the oldest winner of the World Drivers' Championship during the 1970s?

19. How many different teams won races during the 1970s? a) nine b) 11 c) 13

20. Which driver won the most Grand Prix races throughout the whole of the 1970s? a) Emerson Fittipaldi b) Niki Lauda c) Jackie Stewart

Quiz 13: Answers

1. 18 points 2. Nico Rosberg 3. Arrows 4. Donington 5. Nico Rosberg 6. Canadian 7. Spa-Francorchamps 8. True 9. Daniel Ricciardo 10. True 11. The Ardennes 12. Max Verstappen 13. Nick Heidfeld 14. Federation Internationale de l'Automobile 15. David Croft 16. Sir Stirling Moss 17. Miami 18. Jarno Trulli 19. c) Sebastian Vettel 20. c) Nine

Quiz 15: Pot Luck

1. Who secured his first win at the 190th attempt at the Sakhir Grand Prix in 2020?

2. After winning the 2013 Australian Grand Prix, who had to wait another 114 Grands Prix before he won his next race?

3. What colour is the circle on the black flag waved at a car that has mechanical trouble indicating that the driver should head to the pits?

4. Which constructor had more than 200 starts between 2008 and 2018 and reached the podium six times but never registered a win?

5. What is the name of Max Verstappen's dad who started more than 100 Formula One races during the 1990s and early 2000s?

6. Which circuit hosted the British Grand Prix five times between 1955 and 1962?

7. In 2018, Red Bull released a limited-edition series of cans that featured the face of which driver?

8. Which 2022 driver has the race number #18?

9. In 1996, the record for the fewest number of cars to finish a race was tied at Monaco. How many cars made the chequered flag?

10. Which Frenchman recorded his only Grand Prix win in that controversial 1996 race?

11. What was the name of the 2013 film biopic about the rivalry between James Hunt and Niki Lauda?

12. Who won 13 races between 1994 and 2008 but never won a World Championship?

13. 'The Chain', the name of the famous theme tune to the BBC's F1 coverage, was recorded by which group?

14. What are the two African countries to have hosted a Formula One Grand Prix?

15. Which Belfast-born driver won the 1983 United States West Grand Prix despite starting 22nd on the grid?

16. True or false – Nico Rosberg is an investor on the German version of the TV show 'Dragons' Den'?

17. By what name is the Autodromo José Carlos Pace circuit more commonly known?

18. How many points does the third-place finisher receive at a Formula One race?

19. During the first phase of qualifying, a driver must be within what percentage of the fastest time in order to start the race? a) 105% b) 106% c) 107%

20. How did Michael Schumacher do in his Formula One debut? a) He won b) He made the podium c) He retired during the first lap

Quiz 14: Answers

1. Jackie Stewart 2. Jochen Rindt 3. Tyrell 4. Emerson Fittipaldi 5. Hesketh 6. Silverstone and Brands Hatch 7. True 8. Ronnie Peterson 9. Mount Fuji 10. Clay Regazzoni 11. Nurburgring 12. 1976 13. McLaren 14. Jackie Stewart, Emerson Fittipaldi and Niki Lauda 15. Gilles Villeneuve 16. Mario Andretti 17. 1971 18. Mario Andretti 19. c) 13 teams 20. b) Niki Lauda

Quiz 16: 1980s

1. In 1980, who became the second Australian to win the World Drivers' Championship?

2. Which 22-year-old Italian set a then record for the youngest driver to gain pole at the American Grand Prix West in 1982?

3. Who were the two men to win three World Drivers' Championships during the 1980s?

4. Which driver won the 1982 World Championship despite winning just one race that season?

5. Nigel Mansell secured his first Grand Prix win in 1985 in a race held at which circuit?

6. In 1984, who became just the second driver in Formula One history to win the World Drivers' Championship without starting on pole in any race?

7. Which driver won at least one race every year between 1980 and 1987?

8. Ayrton Senna won his first Formula One Grand Prix in wet conditions in a 1985 race at which circuit?

9. Which Frenchman won seven races between 1980 and 1983?

10. Which British driver started 83 races between 1983 and 1989 but never managed a podium finish?

11. Who were the two drivers, one Argentinian and one American, over the age of 39 to gain pole during the 1980s?

12. Nigel Mansell's chances of winning the 1986 World Drivers' Championship were scuppered after he suffered a spectacular blowout at which Grand Prix?

13. Who benefitted from Mansell's tyre trouble to win the World Championship that year?

14. Which 12-time Grand Prix winner retired from the sport two races into the 1982 season?

15. Who gained pole in 13 of the 16 races in the 1989 season but finished second in the World Drivers' Championship?

16. Nigel Mansell was one of two drivers from the UK to win a Grand Prix during the 1980s. Who was the other?

17. The last ever United States Grand Prix West was held in 1983. Which Californian city hosted the race?

18. Which Belgian won his first race at the 85th time of asking in the 1989 Canadian Grand Prix?

19. The 16 races during the 1982 season were won by how many different drivers? a) seven b) nine c) eleven

20. Which driver had the most Grand Prix wins during the 1980s? a) Nelson Piquet b) Alain Prost c) Ayrton Senna

Quiz 15: Answers

1. Sergio Perez 2. Kimi Raikkonen 3. Orange 4. Force India 5. Jos 6. Aintree 7. Daniel Ricciardo 8. Lance Stroll 9. Four 10. Olivier Panis 11. 'Rush' 12. David Coulthard 13. Fleetwood Mac 14. Morocco and South Africa 15. John Watson 16. True 17. Interlagos 18. 15 points 19. c) 107% 20. c) He retired during the first lap

Quiz 17: Pot Luck

1. Which Italian started 208 Grand Prix races between 1980 and 1994 but never won any of them?

2. In 1983, who became the first man to win the World Drivers' Championship driving a car with a turbocharged engine?

3. Whose five wins at the Monaco Grand Prix are the most by a British driver?

4. What is the record for the most wins by a driver in a single season?

5. Who are the co-holders of that most wins in a season record?

6. The crowd rushed onto the Silverstone track after the 1992 race to celebrate which driver's victory?

7. Which Las Vegas casino gave its name to a race that hosted Formula One events in 1981 and 1982?

8. Which driver finished 19 of the 22 races on the 2021 calendar but didn't gain a single point?

9. Ferrari hold the record for the most podium finishes in the history of Formula One. Which constructor is second on that list?

10. Who was the last reigning World Champion to retire from the sport?

11. Who replaced Ayrton Senna in the Williams team after the Brazilian's tragic death?

12. Maggots and Becketts are features of which circuit?

13. True or false – Cars are allowed to refuel during a pit stop?

14. Who is the only Colombian driver to win a Formula One race?

15. What feature of a circuit is defined as 'a tight sequence of corners in alternate directions'?

16. Which Formula One driver from the 1970s and 80s later became a politician in his native Argentina and was the Governor of the Santa Fe region?

17. Which 2022 driver has the race number #4?

18. Who was in last position just over halfway through the 2011 Canadian Grand Prix but went on to win the race?

19. How much was the cost cap for each team for the 2022 season? a) $132 million b) $142 million c) $152 million

20. What was the average height of a driver on the 2021 Formula One grid a) 5ft 7in b) 5ft 8in c) 5ft 9in

Quiz 16: Answers

1. Alan Jones 2. Andrea de Cesaris 3. Alain Prost and Nelson Piquet 4. Keke Rosberg 5. Brands Hatch 6. Niki Lauda 7. Nelson Piquet 8. Estoril 9. Rene Arnoux 10. Jonathan Palmer 11. Mario Andretti and Carlos Reutemann 12. Australian 13. Alain Prost 14. Carlos Reutemann 15. Ayrton Senna 16. John Watson 17. Long Beach 18. Thierry Boutsen 19. c) Eleven 20. b) Alain Prost

Quiz 18: 1990s

1. Who won back-to-back World Championships in 1990 and 1991?

2. Who won his 51st and final Grand Prix at the 1993 German Grand Prix?

3. Which future World Champion won his first Grand Prix at the 96th attempt at the 1997 European Grand Prix?

4. At the 1994 Belgian Grand Prix, which Brazilian set a record as the then youngest driver to achieve pole?

5. Nigel Mansell was one of two Britons to win the World Drivers' Championship in the 1990s. Who was the other?

6. Which Italian holds the record for appearing in the most races before earning a point? (clue: he gained his first points in 1994)

7. In 1996, who became the first driver in Formula One history to win four races in his debut season?

8. Which Finn secured his first podium finish at the 73rd attempt in the 1999 German Grand Prix?

9. Who were the two drivers under the age of 30 to win the World Championship during the 1990s?

10. Which home driver won his only British Grand Prix in the 1995 race?

11. Who became just the second German to win a Formula One race after winning the 1997 San Marino Grand Prix?

12. Who reached the podium every year between 1990 and 1998 but won only one race, the Canadian Grand Prix in 1995?

13. True or false – At the 1996 Monaco Grand Prix, only 16 of the 21 starters survived the first lap?

14. At the 1997 Argentine Grand Prix, who became the first 21-year-old to achieve a podium finish?

15. Who was the oldest driver to win the World Championship during the 1990s?

16. Which Brazilian won his sixth and final Formula One race at the Japanese Grand Prix in 1992?

17. Which driver won the most races throughout the whole of the 1990s?

18. Who was the only non-European to win the British Grand Prix during the 1990s?

19. Nigel Mansell's last win was in 1994 at which Grand Prix? a) Australian b) British c) Monaco

20. Who was the only driver to win five successive races during the 1990s? a) Nigel Mansell b) Alain Prost c) Ayrton Senna

Quiz 17: Answers

1. Andrea de Cesaris 2. Nelson Piquet 3. Graham Hill 4. 13 wins 5. Sebastian Vettel and Michael Schumacher 6. Nigel Mansell 7. Caesars Palace 8. Mick Schumacher 9. McLaren 10. Nico Rosberg 11. David Coulthard 12. Silverstone 13. False 14. Juan Pablo Montoya 15. A chicane 16. Carlos Reutemann 17. Lando Norris 18. Jenson Button 19. b) $142 million 20. c) 5ft 9in

Quiz 19: Pot Luck

1. Who won the 2022 World Drivers' Championship?

2. He secured the title following a rain-interrupted race at which Grand Prix?

3. Who was the first F1 driver to beat The Stig's time in Top Gear's 'Star in a Reasonably Priced Car' feature?

4. True or false – Ayrton Senna won the 1988 World Drivers' Championship despite gaining fewer points over the 16 races than rival Alain Prost?

5. Who is the only driver born in Africa to compete in a Formula One race?

6. How did a man called Cornelius Horan gain notoriety during the 2003 season?

7. Which team won their only Constructors' Championship in 1995?

8. Which Grand Prix takes place at the Marina Bay Street Circuit?

9. Lily Muni, a professional golfer on the LPGA Tour is the girlfriend of which 2022 Formula One driver?

10. At which circuit will you find a corner called the 'Curva Parabolica'?

11. In what year did the Red Bull team make their Formula One race debut?

12. Which driver was in the cockpit for the first and last Grand Prix wins for the Benetton team?

13. In relation to Formula One cars what do the initials DRS stand for?

14. Which 2022 driver has the race number 16?

15. Which British driver was the founder of a Monte Carlo hotel called 'Columbus'?

16. In 1984, Keke Rosberg became the first and only winner of which Texan city's Grand Prix?

17. What was the first team to be fined for breaching cost cap regulations?

18. Who holds the record for the most GP starts without registering a podium finish?

19. Between 1999 and 2002 Ferrari had a podium finish in how many consecutive Grands Prix? a) 43 b) 48 c) 53

20. What was Eddie Irvine's given first name? a) Edgar b) Edmund c) Edward

Quiz 18: Answers

1. Ayrton Senna 2. Alain Prost 3. Mika Häkkinen 4. Rubens Barrichello 5. Damon Hill 6. Nicola Larini 7. Jacques Villeneuve 8. Mika Salo 9. Michael Schumacher and Jacques Villeneuve 10. Johnny Herbert 11. Heinz-Harald Frentzen 12. Jean Alesi 13. True 14. Ralf Schumacher 15. Nigel Mansell 16. Riccardo Patrese 17. Michael Schumacher 18. Jacques Villeneuve 19. a) Australian 20. a) Nigel Mansell

Quiz 20: 2000s

1. Michael Schumacher started the decade by winning how many successive World Drivers' Championships?

2. Who was the only other driver to win back-to-back Drivers' Championships during the 2000s?

3. Which Brazilian won his first race at the 123rd attempt at the 2000 German Grand Prix?

4. Who became the first 21-year-old to win a Formula One race after winning the 2008 Italian Grand Prix?

5. True or false – No French driver won a Grand Prix throughout the whole of the 2000s?

6. 14 teams withdrew from which race in 2005 citing safety concerns over tyres?

7. Who were the two Britons to win the British Grand Prix during the 2000s?

8. In 2007, who became the last man to win the World Drivers' Championship in a Ferrari?

9. Which Brazilian was pipped to the 2008 World Drivers' Championship by Lewis Hamilton?

10. Which Briton won his only World Drivers' Championship in 2009?

11. He secured that title driving for which short-lived team?

12. What Italian team was taken over by Red Bull and renamed Toro Rosso for the 2006 season?

13. At the 2006 Bahrain Grand Prix, who became the first driver under the age of 21 to set a fastest lap?

14. Which Finn secured his only Formula One victory after winning the 2008 Hungarian Grand Prix?

15. Sebastian Vettel made his full Formula One debut at the 2007 United States Grand Prix substituting for which driver who had suffered a spectacular crash at the Canadian GP?

16. Who were the two Italian drivers to win a Grand Prix during the 2000s?

17. Which German finished 33 straight races between 2007 and 2009, the most by any driver during the decade?

18. Which Spaniard made the podium for the first time in his 67th race at the 2006 Hungarian Grand Prix?

19. Which of the following drivers won the most Grands Prix during the 2000s? a) Fernando Alonso b) Lewis Hamilton c) Kimi Räikkönen

20. Which constructor won the most World Championships during the 2000s? a) Ferrari b) McLaren c) Renault

Quiz 19: Answers

1. Max Verstappen 2. Japanese 3. Rubens Barichello 4. True 5. Jody Scheckter 6. He invaded the track at the British Grand Prix 7. Benetton 8. Singapore 9. Alex Albon 10. Monza 11. 2005 12. Gerhard Berger 13. Drag Reduction System 14. Charles Leclerc 15. David Coulthard 16. Dallas 17. Williams 18. Nico Hulkenberg 19. c) 53 20. b) Edmund

Quiz 21: Pot Luck

1. The first ever race in the Formula One World Championship took place at what circuit?

2. Lewis Hamilton is one of three drivers to have started more than 200 consecutive Formula One races. Who are the other two?

3. What colour flag is waved at a driver who has been disqualified from a race?

4. Who holds the record for the most races started without ever gaining pole position?

5. Which constructor achieved 15 podium finishes between 1999 and 2005 but never managed to win a race?

6. In 2005, which Jordan driver became the first Indian to take part in a Formula One race?

7. Who holds the record for the most Grand Prix wins by a driver who failed to win the World Drivers' Championship?

8. What number car does Lewis Hamilton drive?

9. On which street circuit is there a particularly challenging part of the course known as the 'Castle Section'?

10. Who was the first Red Bull driver to achieve a podium finish?

11. In 2008, who became the first Polish driver to win a Formula One race?

12. What do the letters stand for in the safety feature known as the HANS Device?

13. Lasting some 4 hours, five minutes, the longest ever Grand Prix race took place in 2011 in which country?

14. Which former Monaco Grand Prix winner became an award-winning wine producer after he retired from motor racing?

15. The Swimming Pool chicane is a feature of which circuit?

16. Brazil is one of two South American countries to have hosted a Formula One Grand Prix. What is the other?

17. True or false – Stirling Moss was the grandfather of supermodel Kate Moss?

18. Which Dutch driver appeared in the 1982 Dutch Grand Prix, moved to sportscars, then returned to Formula One in Japan in 1992, more than 10 years after his last F1 race?

19. Who is the oldest driver to win a Formula One Grand Prix? a) Louis Chiron b) Luigi Fagioli c) Juan Manuel Fangio

20. How old was he when he won the 1951 French Grand Prix? a) 52 b) 53 c) 54

Quiz 20: Answers

1. Five 2. Fernando Alonso 3. Rubens Barrichello 4. Sebastian Vettel 5. True 6. United States Grand Prix 7. David Coulthard and Lewis Hamilton 8. Kimi Räikkönen 9. Felipe Massa 10. Jenson Button 11. Brawn GP 12. Minardi 13. Nico Rosberg 14. Heikki Kovalainen 15. Robert Kubica 16. Giancarlo Fisichella and Jarno Trulli 17. Nick Heidfeld 18. Pedro de la Rosa 19. a) Fernando Alonso 20. a) Ferrari

Quiz 22: 2010s and Beyond

1. The 2010s started with Sebastian Vettel winning how many successive World Drivers' Championships?

2. How old was Vettel when he claimed his maiden World Championship?

3. The first seven rounds of the 2012 season were won by how many different drivers?

4. In 2012 Pastor Maldonado became the first driver from which country to enjoy a Grand Prix win?

5. Maldonado secured that historic triumph at which Grand Prix?

6. The Buddh International Circuit, which hosted Grands Prix in 2011, 2012 and 2013 is in which country?

7. Who became the fourth Australian to win a Formula One race after winning the 2014 Canadian Grand Prix?

8. Which pair of teammates collided on the first lap of the 2016 Spanish Grand Prix, eliminating both from the race?

9. After a 14-year hiatus, who became the first Frenchman to win a Formula One race after taking the 2020 Italian Grand Prix?

10. Who secured his 15th and final Grand Prix victory at the 2012 Brazilian Grand Prix?

11. Max Verstappen's 2021 World Championship-winning car was powered by an engine made by which manufacturer?

12. In 2019, who became the first driver from Monaco to win a Grand Prix?

13. 16 people were injured after a fire broke out at the Williams garage in the 2012 edition of which Grand Prix?

14. Between 2010 and 2022, only two drivers won the British Grand Prix more than once. Lewis Hamilton was one, who was the other?

15. Who won the most Grands Prix throughout the whole of the 2010s?

16. Between 2010 and 2022, who was the only driver to win the Monaco Grand Prix in back-to-back years?

17. Six World Champions appeared during the 2012 season. Which six?

18. Max Verstappen secured his first F1 Championship in the final race of the 2021 season at which Grand Prix?

19. Who was the first Russian to gain a podium finish in a Formula One race? a) Daniil Kvyat b) Vitaly Petrov c) Sergey Sirotkin

20. Lewis Hamilton failed to win the 2016 World Championship despite winning how many races? a) Eight b) Nine c) Ten

Quiz 21: Answers

1. Silverstone 2. Daniel Ricciardo and Nico Rosberg 3. Black 4. Romain Grosjean 5. BAR 6. Narain Karthikeyan 7. Stirling Moss 8. #44 9. Baku 10. David Coulthard 11. Robert Kubica 12. Head and Neck System 13. Canada 14. Jarno Trulli 15. Monaco 16. Argentina 17. False 18. Jan Lammers 19. b) Luigi Fagioli 20. b) 53 years old

Quiz 23: Pot Luck

1. During the 2022 season, how many points were awarded to the driver who finished a race in fifth position?

2. Which legendary driver won 24 of the 52 Grand Prix races he entered?

3. Who holds the record for the most start-to-finish Grand Prix wins?

4. In 2022, who became the first Chinese driver to compete in a Formula One Grand Prix?

5. True or false – During the 2017 season, Lewis Hamilton scored points in every race?

6. What nationality was Bruce McLaren, founder of the McLaren F1 team?

7. 'Pouhon' is a famous corner at which circuit?

8. What was the first Middle East Gulf state to host a Formula One Grand Prix?

9. Who was the first Red Bull driver to win a Grand Prix?

10. The Suzuka circuit is in which country?

11. How old was Damon Hill when he won the 1996 World Drivers' Championship?

12. At just 5ft 2in who was the shortest driver to race in the 2022 Formula One season?

13. True or false – Mark Webber was the owner of a Mediterranean restaurant located at an English pub?

14. Lewis Hamilton holds the record for the most podium finishes by a British driver. Who is second on that list?

15. What colour flag is waved to warn drivers that there's a slow-moving vehicle ahead?

16. True of false – Both editions of the Luxembourg Grand Prix were actually staged in Germany?

17. Since 1991, the Spanish Grand Prix has been staged in which city?

18. In what country was Max Verstappen born?

19. What is the approximate 0-60 mph time for a Formula One car? a) 1.6 seconds b) 2.6 seconds c) 3.6 seconds

20. What was Lewis Hamilton's amazing margin of victory at the 2008 British Grand Prix? a) 48 seconds b) 58 seconds c) 68 seconds

Quiz 22: Answers

1. Four 2. 23 years old 3. Seven 4. Venezuela 5. Spanish 6. India 7. Daniel Ricciardo 8. Lewis Hamilton and Nico Rosberg 9. Pierre Gasly 10. Jenson Button 11. Honda 12. Charles Leclerc 13. Spanish 14. Mark Webber 15. Lewis Hamilton 16. Nico Rosberg 17. Vettel, Button, Hamilton, Räikkönen, Alonso and Schumacher 18. Abu Dhabi 19. b) Vitaly Petrov 20. c) Ten

Quiz 24: Anagrams

1. Anyone Rants

2. Vet Bites Sealant

3. Wheat Millions

4. Ex Entraps Vamp

5. Spartan Oil

6. Hallo Mind

7. Bingo Scorer

8. Lane Smelling

9. Arenas of London

10. Eloquent Spin

11. Just On Bonnet

12. Chemicals Hear Much

13. Dad Vault Orchid

14. Czars Sail On

15. Radical Dice Iron

16. No Rain Lords

17. Kerb Be Warm

18. Sepia Flames

19. Clean Trolls

20. Eagerly Rips

Quiz 23: Answers

1. 10 points 2. Juan Manuel Fangio 3. Ayrton Senna 4. Zhou Guanyu 5. True 6. New Zealander 7. Spa-Francorchamps 8. Bahrain 9. Sebastian Vettel 10. Japan 11. 36 years old 12. Yuki Tsunoda 13. True 14. David Coulthard 15. White 16. True 17. Barcelona 18. Belgium 19. b) 2.6 seconds 20. c) 68 seconds

Quiz 25: Pot Luck

1. Prior to Lewis Hamilton, who was the last Formula One driver to receive a knighthood?

2. Whose 18 podium finishes in 2021 are the most ever by a driver in a single season?

3. The Jeddah Corniche Circuit is located on the coast of which Sea?

4. The Silverstone circuit is in which English county?

5. Who was the last man to win the World Drivers' Championship in a Lotus car?

6. Which constructor secured their maiden Formula One win in the 2021 Hungarian Grand Prix?

7. Prior to the 2022 race, practice for the Monaco Grand Prix traditionally took place on what day of the week?

8. Which reigning World Champion announced his retirement at the end of the 1993 season?

9. Which circuit is nicknamed 'The Green Hell'?

10. The Circuit of the Americas is located in which US state?

11. Denny Hulme is the only driver from which country to win the World Drivers' Championship?

12. Which famous Formula One figure was the subject of a biography called 'A Different Kind of Life'?

13. True or false – Up to and including 2021, Lewis Hamilton had won at least one Grand Prix in every season he competed?

14. Which region of Spain, best known for sherry production, hosted the Spanish Grand Prix from 1986 to 1990?

15. Which driver had the race number 11 during the 2022 season?

16. The shortest driver in the history of Formula One was Italy's Andrea Montermini. How tall was he in feet and inches?

17. Who set the lap record for the Monaco circuit in 2021?

18. Who was the last man to win the World Drivers' Championship for the Tyrell construction team?

19. In inches, how big are tyres on a 2022 F1 car? a) 16in b) 17in c) 18in

20. What flag is waved at a driver to warn a driver about unsportsmanlike behaviour? a) Black and white diagonals b) Black and white stripes c) Black and white quarters

Quiz 24: Answers

1. Ayrton Senna 2. Sebastian Vettel 3. Lewis Hamilton 4. Max Verstappen 5. Alain Prost 6. Damon Hill 7. Nico Rosberg 8. Nigel Mansell 9. Fernando Alonso 10. Nelson Piquet 11. Jenson Button 12. Michael Schumacher 13. David Coulthard 14. Carlos Sainz 15. Daniel Ricciardo 16. Lando Norris 17. Mark Webber 18. Felipe Massa 19. Lance Stroll 20. Pierre Gasly

Made in the USA
Las Vegas, NV
17 June 2023

73558454R00038